Places We Live

Living on a
Mountain

Ellen Labrecque

a Capstone company — publishers for children

Raintree is an imprint of Capstone Global Library Limited, a company incorporated in England and Wales having its registered office at 7 Pilgrim Street, London, EC4V 6LB – Registered company number: 6695582

www.raintree.co.uk
myorders@raintree.co.uk

Edited by James Benefield and Brenda Haugen
Designed by Richard Parker
Original illustrations © Capstone Global Library 2015
Picture research by Jo Miller
Production by Helen McCreath
Originated by Capstone Global Library Ltd
Printed and bound in China

ISBN 978 1 4062 8779 0
18 17 16 15 14
10 9 8 7 6 5 4 3 2 1

British Library Cataloguing in Publication Data
A full catalogue record for this book is available from the British Library.

Acknowledgments
We would like to thank the following for reproduing photographs: Alamy: Francois Werli, 10, Jan Sochor, 5, Peter Jordan_EU, 27, Robert Harding Picture Library Ltd/Ben Pipe, 8, Robert Harding Picture Library Ltd/Jane Sweeney, 12; Corbis: Olivier Coret, 26; Glow Images: Robert Harding/Christopher Rennie, 13; Landov: EPA Photo/Fabrice Coffrini, 9; Newscom: Danita Delimont Photography/William Sutton, 18, EPA/WEDA, 21, Europics, 19, KRT/Karl Mondon, 23; Shutterstock: Bruce Young, 15, Galyna Andrushko, 14, Goodluz, 22, Irina Mos, 11, JuliaLine, 6, kastianz, 4, LuciaP, 24, Mikadun, 25, Oscar Schnell, 17, Pixachi, 16, pryzmat, 20, StevanZZ, cover.

Design Elements: Shutterstock: donatas1205, Olympus.

We would like to thank Rachel Bowles for her invaluable help in the preparation of this book.

Contents

Some words are shown in bold, **like this**. You can find out what they mean by looking in the glossary.

What are mountains?

Mountains are large **landforms**, higher and steeper than hills. A mountain can stand alone with only one **summit**. Or, a mountain can be part of a row of mountains, which is called a mountain range.

The Andes are a mountain range in South America.

Over 50,000 people live in La Rinconada.

Many people live in **settlements** on mountains, from small farms to cities. The highest city in the world is La Rinconada, Peru, in the Andes Mountains. It is 5,100 metres (16,732 feet) above the sea.

How mountains are formed

Mountains are found all over the world, even under the ocean. Some formed when volcanoes erupted. Mount Elbrus, Russia, was formed this way. It rises 5,642 metres (18,510 feet) into the air.

Mount Elbrus is the largest mountain in Europe.

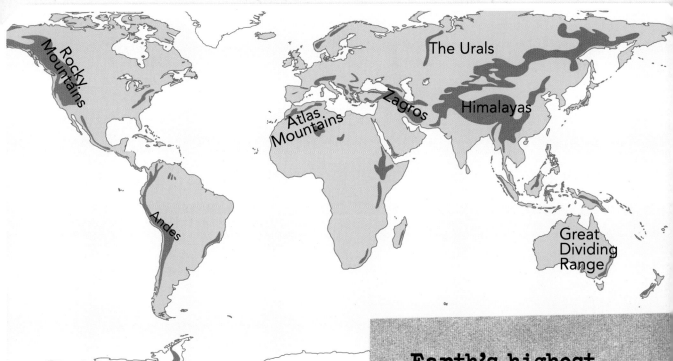

The Urals

Rocky Mountains

Atlas Mountains

Zagros

Himalayas

Andes

Great Dividing Range

Some mountains formed over thousands of years when slabs of Earth's **crust** moved and pushed up giant folds and blocks of land. The Rockies, the Andes, the Himalayas and the Alps are all mountain ranges that were made this way.

Earth's highest mountains

1. Mount Everest, Himalaya range, Nepal and Tibet: 8,850 metres (29,035 feet)

2. K2, Karakoram range, Pakistan and China: 8,611 metres (28,251 feet)

3. Kanchenjunga, Himalaya range, India and Nepal: 8,586 metres (28,169 feet)

Living on a mountain

Daily living on a mountain can be tough. The weather can be windy and cold. The higher you live, the colder it is and the less air there is to breathe. The weather can also change suddenly.

Some mountains have snow on their peaks all year around.

Avalanches and landslides can hurt or even kill people.

Mountain weather can be deadly. **Landslides** and **avalanches** happen without warning. Rocks, soil and snow are set loose by heavy rain and wind and sent crashing downwards.

All kinds of people

One of every 12 people on Earth lives on a mountain. Many **communities** are **isolated**. It is hard to get supplies, such as food and clothes. People here graze animals, or work in forests or mines.

People who live in the mountains of Nepal keep buffalo.

Some homes in Vail cost millions of pounds!

Some people live on mountains for pleasure. They live there because it is beautiful and they enjoy what mountain life can offer. Vail, Colorado, USA, is one of the richest mountain towns in the world.

Clothes and shelter

You have to be ready for all kinds of weather on mountains. People wear layers of clothes that are warm to stop them from getting cold in the chilly mountain air. Sometimes these are made from animal skin and fur, such as from yaks.

Wool from mountain animals makes very warm clothing.

Some **remote** villages in Japan are famous for their houses with sloped roofs.

Mountain homes also have to be ready for bad weather. They have tall, sloping roofs, so that heavy snow, ice and rain slides right off, keeping the people inside safe.

Mountain farmers

Some mountain people are farmers, but farming up high can be hard. Mountain soil is rocky and thin, and the growing season is short. The ground slopes steeply so people can't grow a lot of food.

Farmers make steps into the mountain to make level ground.

These mountain animals also provide milk for the farmer.

Mountain farmers rely on animals such as yaks to help them farm. These animals have rubbery pads on their feet so they don't slip on the rocks. They help people carry loads up and down mountains.

Getting around

Some people in **isolated** mountain **communities** walk to get around. But many people travel up and down mountains in cars. Guard rails are sometimes built along roads to make them safer.

Mountain roads are built to zigzag, so they won't be too steep.

You get a great view if you travel in a cable car!

Some mountains have trains that take people up and down. For example, **commuters** in Switzerland take the train up and along the Alps. Cable cars carry **tourists** over the Blue Mountains in Australia.

What is school like?

Some mountain schools are just like your school. But some pupils enjoy smaller classes and more attention from teachers. There are not as many pupils as there are in more crowded areas.

In the Scottish Highlands some school classes have as few as seven pupils.

In Gangluo County, China, some schools are in mountain caves.

In some **remote** mountain places, going to school is scary! Children who live in Gangluo County, China, go to school 2,800 metres (9,186 feet) above sea level. They have to climb steep steps up a mountain to get there.

What is work like?

Many everyday jobs, such as being a plumber, are found in mountain places. But growing food and taking care of animals such as goats and sheep, can be a full-time job.

Some jobs on mountains are just like jobs anywhere else.

People work on mountains to dig for precious stones and other materials.

Other mountain jobs are **unique**. Mountains are rich in **minerals**, such as gold. Miners dig these out of mountains. People also work as guides. In Nepal's mountains, Sherpas help climbers carry their supplies and act as guides.

Fun things to do

Some people love the things you can do on a mountain. Many people love to hike and climb on mountains to relax, from **tourists** to people who live nearby. They enjoy the views from the top and looking at nature.

Mountain walking can be anything from a gentle hike to a tough climb.

You can mountain bike for fun or as part of a competition.

Mountains are also used for sport. In the summer, they are popular places for people who ride mountain bikes. In the winter, people come to mountains for skiing and other winter sports, such as snowboarding.

23

Mountains of the past

Mountains change over millions of years. They are worn down by wind, water, frost and ice. Mountains in the Scottish Highlands were once high and jagged. Over thousands of years, they **eroded** into lower hills.

The process of wearing down mountains over time is called erosion.

People still explore mountains today!

People in the past have climbed mountains to explore unknown places. Explorers have risked their lives and died searching for new lands. Even today, people climb new peaks to discover things.

Mountains of the future

Humans have damaged mountains. For example, mining has polluted mountain air, soil, streams and animal homes. Also, people have cut down too many trees for wood or to make room for **crops** and cattle.

When there are no trees on mountains, the soil washes away.

Using solar panels means using less firewood. This means cutting down fewer trees.

There are ways we can save mountains. For example, some people plant new trees. Solar panels are also being built high on mountain tops. These panels collect energy from the sunlight to make electricity.

Fun facts

- The Andes in South America is the world's longest mountain range.

- The Alps is probably Europe's most visited mountain range. The Alps is known for winter sports but also for beautiful views.

- The 2014 Winter Olympics took place in the Caucasus Mountains in Sochi, Russia.

- People who climb mountains for fun are called mountaineers.

- There are mountains buried under the ice in Antarctica.

- Most of the world's fresh water comes from mountains.

- The highest mountain in the Solar System is on Mars. It is 25 kilometers high (15.5 miles).

Quiz

Which of the following sentences are true? Which are false?

1. Only rich people live on mountains.

2. There are no cities on mountains.

3. Mountains are not good places for sport.

4. Mountains can change over time.

5. Mining is good for mountains.

1. False. Both rich and poor people live on mountains.

2. False. There are many cities on mountains.

3. False. Sports such as skiing and mountain biking all take place on mountains.

4. True. Mountain can erode over thousands of years.

5. False. Mining can do a lot of damage to mountains.

29

Glossary

avalanche mass of snow, ice or rock falling down a mountain

community group of people or animals who share the same things, such as where they live

commuter person who travels a long way to get to work

crop plants grown by people for food

crust outer layer of the earth which is broken into large slabs, known as plates, that slowly move

eroded when land or rock has been worn or ground down over time by water, ice, snow or wind

isolated place or person that is a long way away from other places or people

landform type of landscape such as hills, mountains, rivers, valleys, cliffs or ridges

landslide sliding down of the earth and rock on a mountainside

mineral special type of rock, sometimes precious, that is found in the ground

remote place far away and not near anything else

settlement place where people live permanently, such as a village, town or city

summit highest part of a mountain

tourist person who visits another place for fun

unique one of a kind; not like anything else

Find out more

Books

Mountains (Learning About Landforms), Chris Oxlade
(Raintree, 2014)

The World's Most Amazing Mountains, Michael Hurley
(Raintree, 2009)

Where on Earth are Mountains, Bobbie Kalman
(Crabtree Publishing, 2014)

Websites

www.bbc.co.uk/learningzone/clips/topics/primary/
geography/mountains.shtml

This BBC website has lots of extra facts about mountains.

www.primaryhomeworkhelp.co.uk/mountains.htm
This website features much more about mountains, from
different types of mountains to beautiful photographs.

www.worldwildlife.org/habitats/mountains
This World Wildlife Fund site is great for learning about
mountains and the animals that live on them.

Index